COMPACT LIVING

March 2006
ISBN 9077213546

PUBLISHER
BETA-PLUS Publishing
Termuninck 3
B - 7850 Enghien (BELGIUM)
T. +32 (0)2 395 90 20
F. +32 (0)2 395 90 21
www.betaplus.com
betaplus@skynet.be

PHOTOGRAPHY
Jo Pauwels a.o. (page 208)

GRAPHIC DESIGN
POLYDEM
Nathalie Binart

TRANSLATION
Laura Watkinson

March 2006
ISBN 9077213546

© All rights reserved. No part of this publication may be reproduced or transmitted in any form or by any means, electronic or mechanical, including photocopy, recording or any other information storage and retrieval system, without prior permission in writing from the publisher.

LEFT PAGE
A project by interior architect *Marc Thoen*.

NEXT PAGES
A modern city apartment, renovated by *In Store*.

CONTENTS

9 | Foreword

14 | PART I: INSPIRING PROJECTS

16   A view of the Thames
24   Light and space in a duplex apartment on the coast
38   Contemporary renovation of a bungalow
46   Revitalisation of a gloomy city apartment
62   Complete renovation of a city apartment
74   Lavish attention to detail
86   A loft apartment above a retail property
96   *Villa Hector*: a compact B&B
102   Contemporary design at the seaside
110   Coastal atmosphere

118 | PART II: COMPACT LIVING IN THE CITY

- 120   Distinctive loft for an art lover
- 128   *Tableau vivant*
- 140   A compact holiday home on the Côte d'Azur
- 152   Using visual simplicity to create space
- 162   A penthouse with a young feel
- 172   A compact total design
- 182   Colourful and surprising
- 190   A metropolitan flat

200 | Addresses

208 | Picture credits

FOREWORD

Compact living is a necessity for some people, but for many it is a conscious choice.

Not only single people, but increasing numbers of young families and dynamic older people are now choosing apartments or city homes with modest proportions.
This makes it all the more important to use the available space efficiently.

This book presents a multitude of useful, space-saving ideas in eighteen projects created by leading interior architects and designers.
Their innovations, often ingenious and sometimes also very simple, can transform a property with a limited amount of space into an exceptionally comfortable home.

Wim Pauwels
Publisher

LEFT PAGE
An *Olivier Dwek* project.
Interior design by *Esther Gutmer*.

NEXT PAGES
This London apartment with its magnificent view of the Thames was designed by *Gilles de Meulemeester* and created by his company *Ebony*.

PART 1

INSPIRING PROJECTS

A VIEW OF THE THAMES

This apartment on the Thames in a building by *Richard Rogers* serves as a pied-à-terre. *Gilles de Meulemeester* was invited to create a light, comfortable atmosphere in this home. The custom-built work was designed by *Ebony Interiors*, with personalised furnishings supplemented by pieces from the *Promemoria* and *Interni* collections.

The materials selected were mainly leather, stained oak, bronze, transparent canework and wool and linen carpets, which worked together with the colour palette perfectly selected by *Gilles de Meulemeester* to give this project a warm and spacious feeling.

P. 16-19

The layout is designed to function around the wonderful view over London. A warm atmosphere has been created in the sitting area through the use of dark woods, fabrics and bronze; the dining room is lighter with its pale shades of wood and the cream-coloured leather.

In the sitting area: *Beau Rivage* sofas, *Loren* armchairs, *Houston* tables, armless *Manhattan* chair and pouf. Art by *Christine Nicaise*.

The original *Bulthaup* kitchen. *Ebony* designed a new central island with storage space in maple and bluestone.

The console and stool in stained oak were specially made by *Ebony*. *Reflets* mirror and a *Brighton* lamp.

LEFT PAGE
A *Bristol* table, *Caffè large* sideboard and chairs. *Reflets* mirror, *Milleraies* carpet and a *Move* lamp.

INSPIRING PROJECTS | 21

The three bedrooms were designed to have a warmer feel: a bronze-coloured linen carpet, fitted furniture and beds in stained oak and swamp oak, a sofa-bed and armchair in natural linen, leather stools and wooden blinds.

The main bedroom (top photo): *Patience* bed and console by *Ebony*.
Gacy armchair and *Achille* stool. *Linen rib* carpet. Art by *Christine Nicaise*.

The guest bedroom (bottom photo): sofa-bed and wardrobe in dark-tinted oak and swamp oak, both specially created by *Ebony*.
Linen rib carpet. *Postpack* artworks by *Christine Nicaise*.

The three bathrooms, which have no natural light, were given extra luminosity through the use of a sandblasted mirror, light tiles and stainless steel.

EBONY
    Gilles de Meulemeester
    av. Louise 132
    B – 1050 Brussels
    T +32 (0)2 646 86 02
    F +32 (0)2 649 52 61
    www.ebony-interiors.com

LIGHT AND SPACE IN A DUPLEX APARTMENT ON THE COAST

Two smaller seaside flats were converted by *Virginie & Odile Dejaegere* to make one large apartment: a holiday home with a simple design that corresponds perfectly to the needs of a young family with children.

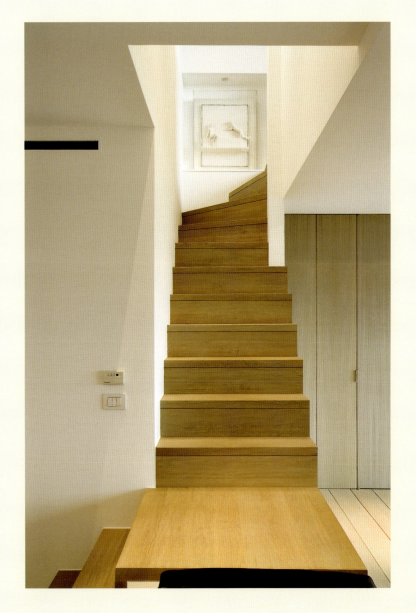

P. 24-25

The new staircase links the two apartments.

LC2 sofas designed by *Le Corbusier* in the sitting room, where the white and beige shades are in keeping with the nearby North Sea.

The parquet floor (planks of 28 cm width) and the fitted cupboards are made of oak that has been given a light stain.

P. 28-29

Chairs and stools by *Harry Bertoia* for *Knoll* in the compact, but practically designed, kitchen-cum-dining area. All lighting in this apartment is by *Modular*.

P. 30-31

The floor and the work surface in the kitchen area are made of composite stone. Simple treatments have been chosen for the windows (white linen curtains) and the walls as well (plain white throughout, painted onto canvas).

P. 32-33

Large, ceiling-height pivoting doors separate the rooms. Maximum use has been made of the available floor space throughout this apartment, but there is still an impression of spaciousness.

Inspiring projects | 33

P. 34-35

As in the bedroom (p. 32-33), the bathroom cupboards have been finished in a wood print, a warm contrast with the white-beige tadelakt walls. Pebbles were chosen for the flooring.

DEJAEGERE

Virginie & Odile Dejaegere
Vaartstraat 25
B – 8500 Kortrijk
T +32 (0)56 22 87 81
F +32 (0)56 20 49 93
MOB. +32 (0)475 79 13 78
www.interiors-dejaegere.be
dejaegere_interiors@hotmail.com

CONTEMPORARY RENOVATION OF A BUNGALOW

Interior architect *Philip Simoen* was asked to convert this 1960s bungalow into a modern home for a young couple.

In spite of the limited dimensions of the building, *Simoen* has still succeeded in creating a new home with an open and spacious atmosphere.

The sitting room in the old part of the house. Black leather seating by *Zanotta*. *Modular* lighting and vintage lamps from the 1970s. Red *Picnik* seating-table combination created by *Xavier Lust* for *Extremis*.

Double fireplace in the sitting area and kitchen. Lighting by *Modular* and a rocking chair by *Eames* for *Vitra*. Illuminated *Ice Cube* bench by *Extremis*. The ceramic composition is by *Anne Meersman*.

The kitchen, a *Philip Simoen* design, has been installed in the new extension.
Fitted white Formica and wengé units. *Smeg* appliances.
Plastic Chair seating (design: *Eames* for *Vitra*, from *Loft Living*) around a stainless-steel dining table.
Modular lighting and a daylight strip between the old and new sections of the house.

The former attic has been converted into a bedroom, dressing room and shower room with fitted MDF cupboards.
Shower in blue 2x2 *Bisazza* glass mosaic tiling (from *Dominique Desimpel*). *Aktiva* fittings from *Grohe*. Steel staircase specially made by *Feys*.

The bathroom has been clad throughout with white glass mosaic tiles from *Bisazza* (2x2 cm). Custom-made washstand with *Axor* tap and *Duravit* basin.

PHILIP SIMOEN
Interior architecture
St.- Sebastiaanstraat 9
B - 8490 Varsenare
T +32 (0)50 388 071
F +32 (0)50 39 23 81
simoen.interieur@telenet.be

REVITALISATION OF A GLOOMY CITY APARTMENT

This apartment in the city initially presented rather a lot of difficulties, including the large number of small, dark rooms. *Pas-Partoe Interieur* took on the challenge of transforming this neglected property into a light, spacious and modern home.

In consultation with architect *Karel Beeck* (who supervised the structural work), a number of interior walls were demolished in order to create a large living room with a dining area on the ground floor. The large folding doors and outside lighting make the garden seem part of the living area. All of the doors were designed to be ceiling height; obtrusive elements such as radiators and loudspeakers have been camouflaged. The limited number of bulky items of furniture has the effect of making the space seem larger. Finally, the contrasts in style, shape and colour reinforce the individual character of this interior.

P. 48-49

The sitting area is next to the kitchen-cum-dining area. A specially made chair, an astrakhan carpet, a corner chair and a *Minotti* pouf. The white-painted wooden blinds have been subtly integrated into the wall.

The anodised aluminium TV unit houses the music system and CD collection.

Above

In the background, *Gandia Blasco* garden furniture. The dining-room chairs and lighting by *J. Morisson* contrast with the simple dining table, which is made from American walnut. The bench is a design by *Bataille & ibens*. The kitchen appliances are kept out of sight behind revolving and sliding doors. Floor of wide bleached Canadian pine planks.

Left page

The *Pawson* kitchen-cum-dining area (installed by *Obumex*) was specially adapted for this space.

LEFT PAGE

View of the master bedroom with a lamp by *Marcel Wanders* in the centre. Door handles in solid nickel-plated brushed brass. The old wooden floor (around 400 years old) has been restored.

P. 54-55

An *Orizzonti* bed with a *Bataille & ibens* bench behind it and a *TO7* wardrobe.

Simple aluminium beds for the children. As in the living room and other spaces, the dark colour adds extra depth. The doors are ceiling height. Sisal flooring.

LEFT PAGE
View of the children's room with its MDF-panel floor, laid in strips and finished with six layers of boat varnish.

Installing the bath below floor level increases the horizontal feel.

LEFT PAGE

The open bathroom with built-in cupboard and washstands by *Vincent Van Duysen*.

Walk-in shower with built-in recess. Taps by *Boffi*. The asymmetry of the washstands, the spot illumination of the white bathroom furniture and the ceiling-height doors give emphasis to this compact space.

PAS-PARTOE
    F. de Merodestraat 27-29
    B – 2800 Mechelen
    T. +32 (0)15 21 12 86
    www.pas-partoe.be
    info@pas-partoe.be

COMPLETE RENOVATION OF A CITY APARTMENT

Instore, the Brussels interior-architecture company, was responsible for the complete renovation of two small apartments to make one larger home with two bedrooms in Bosvoorde (Brussels).

A sofa by *B&B Italia* (model: *Marcel*).

P. 64-65
The impressive music room with wall-to-wall shelving by *Poliform*.

The chair and footstool is a *Vitra* classic.
The low table is by *Knoll*. Couch by *Maxalto*.

ABOVE AND P. 70-71

Metropolitan chairs by *B&B Italia* around a dining table by *MDF Italia* (model: *Keramik*).

INSTORE
    rue Tenbosch 90-92
    B – 1050 Brussels
    T +32 (0)2 344 96 37
    F +32 (0)2 347 59 59
    www.instore.be
    info@instore.be

The small amount of available space has been used optimally in this bedroom and bathroom. The light shades create a strong feeling of spaciousness.

LAVISH ATTENTION TO DETAIL

This duplex apartment was designed by interior architect *Stavit Mor* in close collaboration with *Obumex*: this is a project that gives off a feeling of peace and serenity, with attention being paid in every room to the look of the home as a whole, but with the main focus on a sophisticated sense for details. This is a seaside apartment that is used as a permanent home. The interior architect wanted to create a maritime atmosphere. Light colours and warm materials were chosen, complemented by a number of darker accents.

The doors can be opened throughout this duplex apartment: every room flows seamlessly into the next.

Above the sofa is a work by *Christine Nicaise*. The poufs under the wooden table are made of woven leather. The linen carpet creates a warm atmosphere. The wooden panelling and floors have been finished in the same shade so as to create a feeling of space. *Promemoria* chairs around a circular table from the collection of *Christian Liaigre*.
The drawers are a design by *Stavit Mor*, made by *Obumex*.

Left page
The dark-tinted furniture contrasts with the light interior.

The stairs, which used to be an open staircase, have been fully integrated. This creates a more serene atmosphere and additional storage space. The handrail has been built into the wall to save space.

P. 78-81

The practical *Long Island* kitchen by *Obumex* with its eating area by the window and terrace makes optimal use of the light by the seaside. The vase on the round table is by *Anna Torfs*.

P. 82-83

The leather and wood *Promemoria* console conceals the radiator.

STAVIT MOR

Lambermontplaats 17
B – 2000 Antwerp
T +32 (0)3 230 16 19
stavit.mor@skynet.be

OBUMEX

Showroom Staden
Diksmuidestraat 121
B - 8840 Staden
T +32 (0)51 70 50 71

Showroom Antwerp
L. de Waelplaats 20
B - 2000 Antwerp
T +32 (0)3 238 00 30

Showroom Brussels
Waterloolaan 30
B - 1000 Brussels
T +32 (0)2 502 97 80

Showroom Knokke
Sparrendreef 83
B - 8300 Knokke
TEL.: +32 (0)50 601 666

www.obumex.be
design@obumex.be

The study can also be used as a guest room. Chair from the *JNL Editeurs* collection. Suede and silk bedspread made to a design by *Stavit Mor*.

LEFT PAGE

The use of white marble and mirrored cupboards creates light and space in the bathroom.

A LOFT APARTMENT
ABOVE A RETAIL PROPERTY

Above a retail property, under the slope of the roof, interior architect *Marc Thoen* has created this private apartment with its large adjoining closed terrace.

Sections of the exterior wall have been demolished to bring the living area into direct contact with the terrace. A light stainless-steel window construction with sections that pivot outwards and a wooden floor that links inside and outside combine to create an open, spacious feel.

P. 86-89
Two cupboard units have been subtly integrated alongside the specially made fireplace, which uses either gas or wood. The whole section is mounted on a suspended hand-polished concrete support that was cast on site.
Maxalto seating – *Sity B&B*. Lighting: *Delta Light*. The wide, solid planks of the floor are made of oiled angelin wood.

P. 90-91

The kitchen area has also been opened up to become part of one large living space, like the terrace.

In spite of the relatively small surface area, the use of simple materials and colours creates a larger, more spacious feel.

Above the suspended cooking area, made of a solid *Bruynzeel* surface, is an electric sliding panel that conceals a large storage space. The units are made of wengé veneer and stainless steel. All of the working areas have been given stainless-steel surfaces. The suspended counter has a wengé veneer surface. *Dornbracht* taps, kitchen equipment by *Miele* and *Gaggenau*. Stools: *Mobles 114 Barcelona*. The kitchen was fitted by *Grando*.

A pivoting corridor-width door panel leads into the living area. Extra-long *Maxalto* table. *Zanotta* chairs and *Sity* armchair by *B&B*.

MARC THOEN

Interior architect
Stationsdreef 209
B – 8800 Roeselare
T +32 (0)51 24 84 71
F +32 (0)51 24 84 72
thoen.marc@skynet.be

VILLA HECTOR: A COMPACT B&B

Villa Hector is a house with lots of character. Built in 1892 in the centre of Knokke, it was recently redesigned as a bed and breakfast by *Flamant Projects*.

To the left, a custom-made dresser based on a model from the *Flamant* collection (*Balmore* bookcase). The white of the walls and curtains makes the room appear larger. A *Montreal* sofa, a woollen *Crazy Stone* carpet, a coffee table in *Dunkerque* bluestone and, to the right, a *Twist* standard lamp.

LEFT PAGE

Techniques for increasing the sense of space in the hallway: translucent shades of white (*Flamant Most White* paint), the symmetry of the wainscoting (in *Copenhagen Blue*) throughout the length of the hall with *Navy* cushions and *Laura* wall lamps...

Custom-built *Vancouver* kitchen in bluestone and natural oak. Wall clad with warm-red zelliges. Blinds with wooden slats.

LEFT PAGE

Optimal use of space: a specially made dresser based on the *Long Island* design from the *Flamant* collection. The panelling has been incorporated into the dresser design. *Treviso* light with white linen shade. *Dauphine* chairs around a white *Newport* table.

Califfe washstand; white mosaic shower wall.

FLAMANT PROJECTS
T +32 (0)54 41 54 75
www.flamant.com

B&B VILLA HECTOR
Albertlaan 15
B - 8300 Knokke
MOB +32 (0)475 98 20 30
www.villahector.be

LEFT PAGE

A cosy feeling in the bedroom with its *Bord de Seine* and *Most White* shades. *Rennes* table, *Anna* armchair covered with natural linen, beige *Crazy Stone* carpet.

A *Cape Cod* four-poster bed. *Sara* bed linen and tall *Martine* table lamps. In the foreground is a *Cube* pouf in white linen.

CONTEMPORARY DESIGN AT THE SEASIDE

The Brussels based interior-architecture company *Instore* was responsible for the interior design of this apartment in Knokke-le-Zoute.

LEFT PAGE

The red couch is a *Claire Bataille* design.

Hudson chairs by *Emeco*, designed by *Philippe Starck* in aluminium.

INSTORE
rue Tenbosch 90-92
B – 1050 Brussels
T +32 (0)2 344 96 37
F +32 (0)2 347 59 59
www.instore.be
info@instore.be

P. 106-109
Module sofas *Groundpiece* by *Flexform*.

COASTAL ATMOSPHERE

This apartment, situated in Knokke-le-Zoute, has been realized by the Brussels company for interior design *Instore*.

All cupboards made-to-measure by *Instore* and manufactured in treated, sandy oak, creating a worn aspect, used by the sun, the wind and the sea.

Small *Flexform* chairs (model *Carlotta*).

INSPIRING PROJECTS

P. 112-115
Magnum sofas by *Flexform* around a *Catena* table (*Casamilano*).

INSTORE
rue Tenbosch 90-92
B – 1050 Brussels
T +32 (0)2 344 96 37
F +32 (0)2 347 59 59
www.instore.be
info@instore.be

P. 116-117
Custom-made kitchen by *Instore*. Clothes /coat hooks *Zanotta*.

Inspiring projects | 115

PART II

COMPACT LIVING IN THE CITY

DISTINCTIVE LOFT FOR AN ART LOVER

This distinctive loft has been created by the Brussels based company for architecture and interior design *Olivier Dwek*.

The furniture has been carefully selected by *Esther Gutmer* in full harmony with the interior and the owner's collection of contemporary art.

The red lamp is from *Instore*.

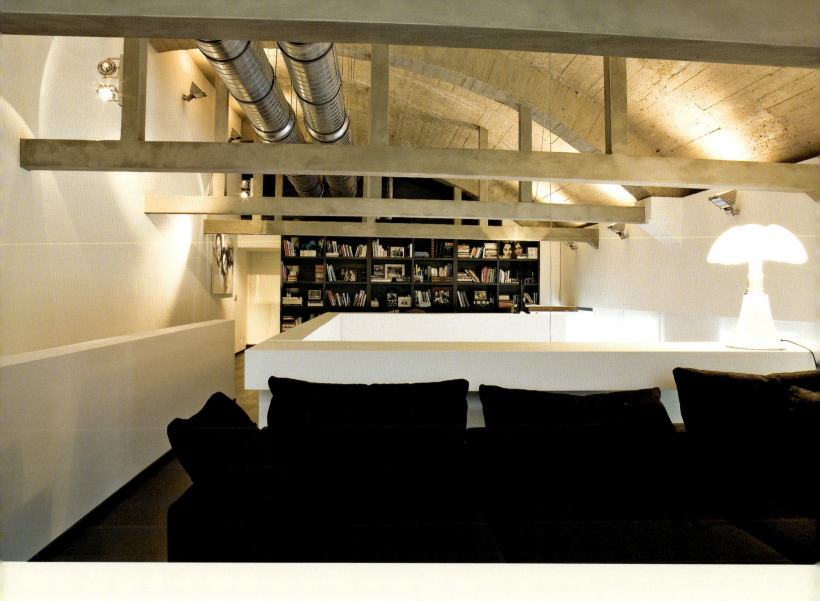

OLIVIER DWEK

Architecture and interior design
av. Brugmann 34
B – 1060 Brussels
T +32 (0)2 344 28 04
F +32 (0)2 344 28 00
MOB +32 (0)475 666 100
dwek.architectes@gmail.com

MEG

Esther Gutmer
av. Klauwaerts 27
B - 1050 Brussels
T +32 (0)2 648 25 00
F +32 (0)2 648 18 06
e.gutmer-meg@skynet.be

TABLEAU VIVANT

Olivier Dwek created this apartment for an enthusiastic collector of modern art, basing the design around her art collection.

The large window sections ensure a close link with the trees in the avenue outside, producing real *tableaux vivants*.
All of the sliding doors can be integrated into the walls, which gives this project a character that lies somewhere between a loft and an apartment.
The decoration was carried out by the owner of the house.
Project realized in collaboration with interior architect *Coline Visse*.

The pivoting panels create a surprising effect. The entrance to the guest lavatory and the bedroom corridor are concealed behind the cupboards.
The photo in the alcove is by *Jean-Marc Bustamante* (*Cyprès*). An urn by the Finnish sculptress *Erna Aaltonen* (from *Philippe Denys* gallery). The artwork in the corridor is by *William Wegman* (*Galerie Xavier Hufkens*).

NEXT PAGES
The central block is a freestanding element that creates a visual partition between the dining room and the sitting area, but ensures that these spaces are still seen as one unit. To the left is a work by *Chan Gha Wang*. A 1946 Platform bench by *George Nelson*.

The large windows ensure a close link with the surrounding nature. Three-legged *Costes* chairs by *Philippe Starck*. Art by *Robert Mangold*, *Thomas Schütte* and *Moshekwa Langa*. Two padded *Barcelona* seats by *Mies van der Rohe* from *Knoll*.

NEXT PAGES
The suspended wall above the fireplace can also be used as a projection screen for video pieces. *Zanotta* sofas. The white work of art is by *Fontana*.

A multimedia piece by *Wim Delvoye* in the study.

The cupboards in the entrance hall conceal the entrance to the guest lavatory and the bedroom corridor. To the right, *Orchids* by photographer *Robert Mapplethorpe*.

LEFT PAGE

The *master bedroom*. The sliding doors with brushed stainless-steel handles make it possible to close the room completely or to open it up. Art by *Roni Horn* and *Ettore Spalletti*. A rocking chair by *Zanotta*. Lamp by *Sabino*.

The main bathroom was designed by the architectural firm of *Olivier Dwek* and built in grey Italian stone, Grigio Adriatico, by *Lapidis*. Taps: *Dornbracht*.
Shower with integrated hammam system.
The dressing room was specially created by *Dwek* in dark-tinted oak.

OLIVIER DWEK
    Architecture & interior design
    av. Brugmann 34
    B – 1060 Brussels
    T +32 (0)2 344 28 04
    F +32 (0)2 344 28 00
    MOB. +32 (0)475 666 100
    dwek.architectes@gmail.com

A COMPACT HOLIDAY HOME ON THE CÔTE D'AZUR

Small in size, but ingenious in design: this apartment in Cannes offers all the necessary comforts of a holiday home in a space of around 100 m².

P. 140-143

Sphere Home Interiors created an understated atmosphere in this home, where all of the functions flow seamlessly into each other: working, relaxing, watching TV, and so on.

Suede poufs and a couch from the *Meridiani Home Collection*. Art by *An Selen*.

P. 144-147

The kitchen was created to a *Sphere* design. Chairs by *Meridiani*. Pottery by *Vincent Van Duysen*.

P. 148-149

Beds by *Olivier Strelli* for *Beka* and poufs from *Marie's Corner*. *Gwendolino* bed linen and lighting by *Stéphane Davidts*. Cane terrace furniture by *Sempre*.

SPHERE HOME INTERIORS

www.sphere-interiors.be

Turnhoutsebaan 308
B - 2970 Schilde
T +32 (0)3 383 50 67
F +32 (0)3 383 32 51

Bredabaan 197
B - 2930 Brasschaat
T +32 (0)3 651 27 40
F +32 (0)3 651 27 41

MOB.: +32 (0)479 27 47 43

LEFT PAGE

The bathroom, also a *Sphere* design, is clad with marble mosaic. *Dornbracht* taps.

USING VISUAL SIMPLICITY TO CREATE SPACE

This penthouse apartment offers a wonderful view of a park and the city centre.
The original floor plan – with no fewer than fourteen doors – was simplified by interior architect *Marc Thoen* to create a design with two pivoting doors and six fully integrated sliding doors.
The interior design, built around the central stairwell, had to accommodate the reduced mobility of the mother of this young family.
The choice of materials and colours has resulted in a simple and restful look.

All of the technical equipment in this central living space has been replaced: the underfloor heating, the air-circulation system and the lighting have been fully integrated.
In consultation with *Boucherie*, wasted space in the roof was opened up so as to create rooms that were as functional and spacious as possible.

The fitted kitchen, designed by *Marc Thoen*, is made from Basaltina natural stone and matt lacquerwork. Built by *Lefever*.

The parents' bedroom, dressing room and bathroom on the northwest side of the apartment. Bathroom with walk-in shower in Carrara marble mosaic. Suspended Carrara surface with built-in washbasins. Taps: *Cisal*.

LEFT PAGE AND ABOVE

Marc Thoen has created a plain and comfortable atmosphere in this compact space by keeping it simple and choosing a good balance of materials (bleached French oak, wengé, Basaltina stone and white Carrara marble).

A study area in the children's bedroom.

MARC THOEN
Interior architect
Stationsdreef 209
B – 8800 Roeselare
T +32 (0)51 24 84 71
F +32 (0)51 24 84 72
thoen.marc@skynet.be

A PENTHOUSE WITH A YOUNG FEEL

Immediately after completing her studies in interior design, *Magali Van den Weghe* was asked to create a young and modern atmosphere in this thirty-year-old penthouse.

She took a very thorough approach to all aspects of the job: walls were demolished and pipes and cables were rerouted with the aim of making the most of the space and the light. For the same reason, simple lines and shapes in sober materials were used throughout.

A long table with benches was chosen for the dining area so that the space would not be broken up by lots of backrests.
The art by *Muriël Emsens* adds a colourful note.
In the centre is an old crystal chandelier.

To avoid overloading the narrow kitchen, a simple matt lacquer finish was chosen for the cupboards (*MDC meubelen*), with grey basaltina for the floor and surfaces (*Van den Weghe nv*).

P. 166-169

There are no large doorframes and the same flooring runs through from one room into the next to create as spacious an impression as possible.

The walk-in shower, which can be closed off using two frosted-glass doors, can be reached via the bathroom or via the lavatory.
This means that guests can have the use of a special mini-bathroom.

MAGALI VAN DEN WEGHE
Oude Houtlei 108
B - 9000 Ghent
T +32 (0)478 672 372
magali.van.den.weghe@telenet.be

MDC MEUBELEN
Rijksweg 95
B - 9870 Machelen
T +32 (0)9 386 17 93

VAN DEN WEGHE NV
The Stone Company
Statiestraat 69
B - 9870 Zulte
T +32 (0)9 388 83 00
www.vandenweghe.be

A COMPACT TOTAL DESIGN

This "compact total-design project" created by interior architect *Filip Vanryckeghem* and implemented by *Interieur Vandeputte* was developed through constant dialogue with the client: the result is an environment in which the owner feels completely at home and where a pleasant and functional atmosphere has been created in spite of the limited amount of space.

The practical, space-saving design of the dining area.

Left page
The open character of this apartment is already clear from the entrance hall, which is connected to the sitting room.

Next pages
Soft furnishings and window treatments were provided by *Domus*. Paintwork by *A. Vanwalleghem*.

An open design was chosen for the kitchen, which is closely connected both to the dining area and the reception space.

In order to emphasise the unity of the design, the same materials were used for the bathroom and lavatory as for the kitchen: lacquered glass, *Corian* surfaces and fitted carpet (*Kordekor / Oxfloor*).

The open entrance hall alongside the living room has a glass partition that can be used to separate the two areas.

IXTRA

Design – detailed study – coordination
Interior architect: Filip Vanryckeghem
Ieperstraat 18
B – 8930 Menen
MOB. +32 (0)474 311 974
T+F +32 (0)56 53 04 57
www.ixtra.be
info@ixtra.be

COLOURFUL AND SURPRISING

When he designed this apartment with a view of the sea, *Axel Pairon* went for a very colourful, modern look.

The decor is plain and simple, but it's still cosy and the owners of the apartment really feel at home there. This design has a relaxed atmosphere that puts you into a holiday mood the moment you step through the front door.

LEFT PAGE

The mirror, with its playful colours and shapes, is by *Billio Nic*.

Above

The kitchen was designed by *Derek Wilson*.

Left page

The large painting, a work by *Marleen Kunnen*, formed the basis for the adventurous colour combinations that can be found throughout the apartment.

P. 188-189
Every bedroom has its own character. *Axel Pairon* selected the different colours from the same palette and repeated them in all the rooms of the apartment, thereby creating a sense of unity, whilst still employing a range of wonderful materials with different textures and a variety of colours. The bathroom is by *Derek Wilson*.

AXEL PAIRON

Interior design / Antiques
Molenstraat 209
NL-5556 TA Valkenswaard
T +32 (0)498 102 815

A METROPOLITAN FLAT

This apartment, situated in the heart of Brussels, has been redesigned by *Gilles de Meulemeester* and custom-built by *Ebony Interiors*.

Warm tones, sober and noble materials, an intimacy with contemporary and timeless lines, ... this is a project very close to *Gilles de Meulemeester*'s universe.

The library has been custom-made by *Ebony*. A low table *Edouardo* in anthracite grey.

LEFT PAGE
Oak panels dissimulate the elevator and service entrance.

P. 192-193
On the bronze wooden floor a pouf / low table in linen. Custom-made sofas *Manhattan* in natural linen. Chairs in oak and leather by *Promemoria*. American stores in voile linen, curtains in khaki cotton.

P. 194-195
A desk *Nord-Sud*. Armchair and chairs *Promemoria*. A custom-made carpet.

ABOVE

Artwork by *Christine Nicaise*.

An oil on canvas painting by *Florimond Dufoor*. Lamp in wengé / bronzed oak.

LEFT PAGE

A *Dumbo* table and *Marella* chairs, both made of anthracite grey oak.

A buffet with doors and drawers in palisander, a striped woolen carpet, a console table in iron and wengé.

The dressing has been custom-built in bronzed oak. Two doors dissimulate the entrance to the bathroom.

EBONY

Gilles de Meulemeester
av. Louise 132
B – 1050 Brussels
T +32 (0)2 646 86 02
F +32 (0)2 649 52 61
www.ebony-interiors.com

LEFT PAGE
Bed cover and cushions made to measure in linen and silk. A side table in ebony. Art by *Ela Tom*.

The dressing in the main bedroom has been manufactured in tinted oak.

ADDRESSES

DEJAEGERE
Virginie & Odile Dejaegere
Vaartstraat 25
B – 8500 Kortrijk
T +32 (0)56 22 87 81
F +32 (0)56 20 49 93
MOB. +32 (0)475 79 13 78
www.interiors-dejaegere.be
dejaegere_interiors@hotmail.com
p. 24-37

DWEK OLIVIER
Architecture & Interior Design
Brugmannlaan 34
B – 1060 Brussels
T +32 (0)2 344 28 04
F +32 (0)2 344 28 00
MOB +32 (0)475 666 100
dwek.architectes@gmail.com
p. 120-127, p. 128-139

EBONY SPRL
Gilles de Meulemeester
132 avenue Louise
B – 1050 Brussels
T +32 (0)2 646 86 02
F +32 (0)2 649 52 61
www.ebony-interiors.com
p. 16-23, p. 190-195

FLAMANT PROJECTS
T +32 (0)54 41 54 75
www.flamant.com
p. 96-101

INSTORE
rue Tenbosch 90-92
B – 1050 Brussels
T. +32 (0)2 344 96 37
F. +32 (0)2 347 59 59
www.instore.be
info@instore.be
p. 62-73, p. 102-109, p. 110-117

IXTRA
Filip Vanryckeghem
Ieperstraat 18
B – 8930 Menen
MOB. +32 (0)474 311 974
T+F +32 (0)56 53 04 57
www.ixtra.be
info@ixtra.be
p. 172-181

MDC MEUBELEN
Rijksweg 95
B - 9870 Machelen
T +32 (0)9 386 17 93
p. 162-171

MEG
Esther Gutmer
av. Klauwaerts 27
B - 1050 Brussels
T +32 (0)2 648 25 00
F +32 (0)2 648 18 06
e.gutmer-meg@skynet.be
p. 120-127

MOR STAVIT
Lambermontplaats 17
B – 2000 Antwerpen
T +32 (0)3 230 16 19
stavit.mor@skynet.be
p. 74-85

OBUMEX

Showroom Staden

Diksmuidestraat 121

B - 8840 Staden

T +32 (0)51 70 50 71

Showroom Antwerp

L. de Waelplaats 20

B - 2000 Antwerp

T +32 (0)3 238 00 30

Showroom Brussels

Bd de Waterloo 30

B - 1000 Brussels

T +32 (0)2 502 97 80

Showroom Knokke

Sparrendreef 83

B - 8300 Knokke

TEL.: +32 (0)50 601 666

www.obumex.be

design@obumex.be

p. 74-85

PAIRON AXEL

Molenstraat 209

NL-5556 TA Valkenswaard

T +32 (0)498 102 815

p. 182-189

PAS-PARTOE BVBA

F. de Merodestraat 27-29

B – 2800 Mechelen

T. +32 (0)15 21 12 86

www.pas-partoe.be

info@pas-partoe.be

p. 46-61

SIMOEN PHILIP BVBA

Interior architecture

St.- Sebastiaanstraat 9

B - 8490 Varsenare

T. +32 (0)50 388 071

F +32 (0)50 39 23 81

simoen.interieur@telenet.be

p. 38-45

SPHERE HOME INTERIORS

www.sphere-interiors.be

Turnhoutsebaan 308

B - 2970 Schilde

T +32 (0)3 383 50 67

F +32 (0)3 383 32 51

Bredabaan 197

B - 2930 Brasschaat

T +32 (0)3 651 27 40

F +32 (0)3 651 27 41

MOB.: +32 (0)479 27 47 43

p. 140-151

THOEN MARC

Interior architecture

Stationsdreef 209

B – 8800 Roeselare

T +32 (0)51 24 84 71

F +32 (0)51 24 84 72

thoen.marc@skynet.be

p. 86-95, p. 152-161

VAN DEN WEGHE MAGALI

Oude Houtlei 108

B - 9000 Gent

T +32 (0)478 672 372

magali.van.den.weghe@telenet.be

p. 162-171

VAN DEN WEGHE NV

The Stone Company

Statiestraat 69

B - 9870 Zulte

T +32 (0)9 388 83 00

www.vandenweghe.be

p. 162-171

VILLA HECTOR B&B

Albertlaan 15

B - 8300 Knokke

MOB +32 (0)475 98 20 30

www.villahector.be

p. 96-101

LEFT PAGE

A *Marc Thoen* project.

NEXT PAGES

This kitchen has been manufactured by *Obumex*.

PICTURE CREDITS

All pictures: Jo Pauwels, except:

p. 102-117　　　　　　　　Jean-Luc Laloux